D0973630

I AM YOUR SLAVE
NOW DO WHAT I SAY

ANTHONY MADRID

CANARIUM BOOKS
ANN ARBOR, BERKELEY, IOWA CITY

SPONSORED BY
THE UNIVERSITY OF MICHIGAN
CREATIVE WRITING PROGRAM

I AM YOUR SLAVE
NOW DO WHAT I SAY

Canarium Books
Ann Arbor, Berkeley, Iowa City
www.canariumbooks.org

The editors gratefully acknowledge the
University of Michigan Creative Writing Program
for editorial assistance and generous support.

Cover art: Mark Fletcher
Design: Gou Dao Niao

First Edition

Printed in the United States of America

ISBN 13: 978-0-9849471-0-2

CONTENTS

1.

2.

3.

4.

5.

6.

580 STROPHES : LIBRI SEX

EACH AND EVERY TIME THEY LAUNCH
A TRAIN UP THE TUBE

EACH and every time they launch a train up the tube, it costs the
city hundreds of dollars.
Old people often see those hundreds roiling in the air of the
tunnels.

Here he comes again, that eerie torchlit blackbird. They should
not have released him
From the ice he was bound in; they should not have taught him
speech.

Wretched, cross-firing, eleven-leggèd SUN, tutor to kings,
animator of bees,
Leave off threading needles with camels, with double-humped
camels, with double-humped camels!

Summer's coming, with its eight-cylinder musclecar heartbeat.
A shoe-shaped fish, complete with laces, will be caught on the
Gas Pedal Solstice.

And doesn't the old legend say that a woman is always her own
best counsel?
Ah, those bloodthirsty Mexican legends, wherein no one gets any
advice!

Whereas, MADRID is always at the ready with what he calls Golden
Advice.
He says we must write six books, every one of us. Let's begin
with *The Devil's Dictionary*.

BENEATH YOUR PARENTS' MATTRESS

BENEATH your parents' mattress is a stairwell leading
   downward.
That bed is like a door on which your parents knocked to
   summon you.

Moles are a kind of meteor. Their careers are knots in the earth.
Because the earth is a ball, the way out of the maze is straight up.

Punishing young woman, fueled by a river of burning stones,
Put up your black snake whip, set aside your thorny iron ball on a
   stick.

For, if I do not solve, within the next few hours, the eternal
   tormenting mystery of love,
Then let herds of city buses packed with foreigners drive over my
   hollow corpse.

Angels in the bath! But they're not really angels; they're merely girls.
And that water is hardly water. It is the blood in your own ears.

And everything from passion's aphelion to integral calculus is
   telling you to go.
But always you find the hinge of the door on everwhich side you
   pull . . .

MADRID has a black charm-bangle. When he's angry, he rubs the
   black charm-bangle.
Right now his fingers are *white* from how hard he's rubbing the
   black charm-bangle.

THEY HAVE BUILT A PUBLIC FOUNTAIN

THEY have built a public fountain with the stones they threw at
   my father.
I have tasted the water of that fountain; I found it sweet.

Famous cousin, we see you studying that dictionary in deadly
   earnest.
We see you assisted by a single lit filament, in the small hours of
   the morning.

A hornet lives all her life with a multiplex dagger in her vitals.
Who swears to avenge her younger self must fly | through miles
   of empty air.

It's no use counting seeds; they won't all come up. Better say:
"Gardener, they're happy to count themselves, if only you'll stand
   out of their light."

No need for devilish alphabets or for any code whatsoever.
They are right not to play at games who are certain to get no
   pleasure.

MADRID! like you and every other preacher, I am eaten up with
   guilt.
I have eight sacks of lead shot hung about my heart.

CROWS TOO HAVE A MEANS OF PURRING

CROWS, too, have a means of purring. Here is what they do.
They shuffle a deck of cards in their smoking guts.

I shall go into the earth, my child, though my path be blocked
With rocks the size of houses, with gymnasium-sized rocks.

Things subject to mere fashion will be ignored at the Final
    Judgment.
You will not be made to answer for your morality.

When people walk around naked, they all look like people I know.
My tutor taught me long ago that bodies are all the same.

"The male is caught in a cleft stick." Better write thát one down.
Love remains sensual, though designed for seraphic;—

And even MADRID, gone to hell and back, can only be trusted
To be chaste insofar as it is consonant with his pride.

THE TEMPTER WILL GO US ONE BETTER

CROW-in-the-parking-lot knows not to waste words. His mere
    look sticks a
Fork into the would-be lover's hand.

In the afterlife, things are cheap. You can buy a team of oxen for a
    penny.
For a nickel, you can buy two barrels of powder—with match and
    bullet suitable.

O planet-battering working boot, top-full of ass kicks,
Your Gemini lover has run off. Has stepped out of your orbit.

I will tell the disconsolate their business; I will speak roughly.
I will reopen the metal account book with the names all struck
    through.

The plush underlip of the Great Male Beauty is tense, has lost its
    color!
The Great Sensuous Hands are trembling, look! They're turning
    back into hooves.

Comes a day we all go naked; all we say will be understood.
The Tempter will go us one better then. He'll know exactly what
    to do . . .

Aw, cool it, MADRID. Set aside that book of cruelty poetry.
Your sins are all behind you—provided you're backing up.

MOST LIVING CREATURES LEAVE NO GHOST

MOST living creatures leave no ghost, and even if they do it's
  totally useless.
Whereas, one can knock a hole in a brick wall with the ghost of a
  material object.

20 January 2001. A leafless little tree full of egg-shaped sparrows.
And every egg has a dot of blood; every dot, a nebula of extending
  branches.

In Mexico City, I saw a crushed dog skeleton into the asphalt.
The flesh had all turned to tar in the side-splitting sun . . .

Anything that's the product of ten years of misery deserves
  respect. That's why I
Respect this Rorschach grave, these sticky bones . . .

BOOKS that give you plenty of time to yourself are not to be
  scorned.
For don't we all need "just a little time to ourselves"—?

See how the stubborne damzell doth deprave my simple meaning!
She's quick to sniff out insult in every little ambiguous phrase.

Praise is due Mother Nature at this, the start of her new fiscal year.
Silver maple's printing money again; box elder's opened its
  offices . . .

And even MADRID is putting out a few timid tender leaves.
A poem or two to be recited in the presence of the infant Mira.

IN HELL THE UNITS ARE THE GALLON AND THE FUCK

THE unit of wine is the cup. Of LOVE, the unit is the kiss. *That's here.*
In Hell, the units are the gallon and the fuck. In Paradise, the drop and the glance.

Ants are my hero. They debate and obey. They can sit at a table for
Eight hours, drawing. They spot out the under-theorized . . .

Have some. For they are as abundant here as the flecks of mica in
the Iowa night sky.
What are twenty-sided dishes of fancy almonds? What use jewels?

HE is Kālidāsa. YOU are nothing. Or rather, you're a tray of
stainless steel cones.
Meanwhile, one opens *Kumārasambhava* to rainbow-colored
crystals pointing every which way.

Nice try. You're a tank-builder but you refuse to build tanks. And
so now you are to be watched over
By three heckling birds, evilly named, discomfiting to children.

¡Fíjate! you're to be watched by three fowl, commonplace in
Florida. Even these
Three hearty objectionables: the blue tit, the woodpecker, and the
swampcunt.

I'm one to talk. I'm so twisted up, my only hope is Salena. My
physical therapist,
With the eyes of Athena—and the hands of a destroying eagle.

HIS TEARS ARE AS OURS ARE

HIS tears are as ours are: ordinary water. But this blind man's
   tongue is washed
With superhuman venom.

A village cur knows better: he warms himself in ashes.
He may settle among the limbs of a merchant's son.

Musician, approach the throne. Present your many-headed
   instrument.
At my signal, Musician, you are to sing.

On moonless nights, the giant saguaro become their own shadows.
Their spines (porrect, acicular) have only the potency of
   silhouettes.

Magical books have been constructed in abundance. But,
   unhappily,
The magic inheres only in the manuscript.

Your skull (and all that's in it) is an old-fashioned passenger
   balloon.
Mouth and tongue are flame and bellows; the heart, the drifting
   basket.

Here's a snake with two tails and teeth all down its throat.
You have to snatch it off the floor with tongs, launch it headfirst
   into the bag.

These able-bodied lovers! What an afterlife they're earning!
They don't know that, for every embrace, we have to write a
  200-page defense.

I'm gonna throw a rope around this building and haul it up a hill.
I'll bite my teeth into the rope and flex my neck and PULL.

Oh, let the MORON speak his poetry. For in my village it is the
  custom:
Whoever opens his mouth without cunning must in no wise be
  suppressed.

THEIR FULMINATIONS ARE MERE THEATER

THEIR fulminations are mere theater, and their offended morals,
  smoke.
They will people the bottomless pit with their descendants.

You cup in your hands a little white hill of dry Arizona dirt.
The dust exhaling off the top seems steam.

You can only afford one cup? So the two of you will share it.
Who has no money must have recourse to the practice of rapport.

In our tribe, we have recurring days wherein you must travel
  empty-handed.
Exceptions are made for children, of course. And people no better
  than children.

How long must she be your lover before you can recognize her by
  her gait?
By the shuffle of her sandals as she goes up the stairs with your
  rival.

How long must she be your lover before you can hear that it's her,
Though you're in a landing airplane, and she is just stepping out of
  her bath.

Does not the open mouth of a cave sing? It sings, goddamn you.
And each black and fluttering note has its own radar.

One day the DRAGON will ascend angrily from the river down in
  the cave.
Who lives on the mountain will hear the sound of an uncoiling
  battleship chain.

One day the dragon will ascend angrily from the *icy* river in the
  cave.
That fire-breathing dragon that can only be killed by a naked man.

Here's a twenty-year-old girl with a red collared blouse, tight
  jeans, and all the rest of it.
She is not the promised earth, for the EARTH is a fat woman
  wearing a jungle.

Oh, MADRID's out on a limb all right, no question about that.
And down below? A kicked-over three-leggèd stool.

IN THE STONES OF A BULL

WAR-weary general, manfully squinting into the sunlight,
Call back your invincible armies. Show mercy to the heathen
  peoples.

The 580 strophes began as more than a hundred and forty-five
  thousand,
But I have scissored out all the distichs I judged obscene.

In this universe practically naked of reasons to get to know one
  another,
We need every excuse we can get . . .

Young woman walking the road to Rome, with a book of Latin
  poetry in your jacket,
Come over here and read something aloud—to me and to my
  family.

Iguana's no kind of flower: only a muscular row of thorns.
The dewy red petals are elsewhere. Are in | the licking mouth of a
  dog.

I am going into the prayer room; I am intent on saying a prayer. I
  have
Memorized the unrhymed sonnet that begs forgiveness of those we
  love.

In the STONES of a bull stands a House of Representatives.
Togas are still in fashion there—also the ax and the faggot of sticks.

Says MADRID: The buck and the rooster nest in my palm.
Therefore, let the foundation of my fame be my openhandedness.

SHE WANTS TO KNOW WHAT I'M LOOKING AT

SHE wants to know what I'm looking at, so I tell her I'm looking
    at her body.
Seven years now we've been the model of physical love between
    the sexes.

By East Hyde Park Boulevard, I had an impure thought, and I saw a
Sparrow come sailing straight at me like a bullet.

A sparrow's wings can shut down like a beetle's outer case; like a
Snapped-home pocketknife blade is the wing of a bulleting
    sparrow.

My grandfather cleared a place in his yard, dug a hole, and dropped
    a tree in it.
He told us he was just as good as God.

What things must we have found if we had searched that god's
    garden,
That old coalminer's garden in Virginia . . .

Oh, Nadya! come outside with me! let's hold hands and have a look
At our pretty little brown-haired clarinet-playing daughter!

She made a little Baby Jesus and put it in an owl's nest;
Now she wants to set it afloat, but we say no . . .

"Anthony, what can this mean? This language amazes me."
It means I wish I could give you a daughter exactly like yourself.

I WANTED TO BE AN ANGEL

I WANTED to be an angel; I cared nothing for being a man.
And now I am neither—and no use to hardly anybody.

Fix your eye on a word, friend, and all around is unintelligible.
The truth is you're always looking through a tube.

They assume the idea is to get as close as you can get. They forget
The use of the extended arm, the thing it's there to measure.

I believe those who surrender must. That I despise them is true.
But it makes a difference I don't believe in Free Will.

I am reading Sara Teasdale, whose joys were only three:
Caress; create; and gape at mindless Nature.

And, now my work is finished, I am reaching for a match:
A match, which is a little rocket with no place to go . . .

Tch! forget about these things, MADRID. Better turn and face
  forward.
Day is coming. The ground is blue. The sidewalk is slick with
  yellow leaves.

I SHALL SIT ATOP OLYMPUS

I SHALL sit atop Olympus; I shall juggle dying worlds.
I shall trifle with Great Hatreds and toy with Young Love.

So, let the girl from Rose Apple Tree Island bring her famous box
of paints.
Let her set to work with her single-haired paintbrush on the living
face of the Queen.

Not for nothing do we maintain this race of bird-eating royal
spiders.
Each precious abdominal hair follicle has its place in the Cosmetic
Scheme.

Behold our palace foreman, wise in the ways of pleasure. He has a
belt with a
Wheel of revolving dildos, like the lens turret on a microscope.

And when our scientific equipment fails us, we PUNISH it with a
hammer!
In the case of our most advanced equipment, we have to use a
jeweler's hammer.

In my culture, we know the outsiders by the fact they can't
answer our riddles.
"Father's in the room; his beard is outside" is a ready-to-hand
example . . .

But to sharpen his carpenter's pencil, MADRID AL-KATIB has no
need of a knife.

He just sticks it in his mouth and sucks. One SUCK and it's sharp as
a needle.

OF THE MANY HYMNS TO THE GODDESS KALI

OF the many hymns to the goddess Kali, only one is worthy a
    poet's respect.
I mean the one wherein her ankles are hung with severed arms;—

I mean the one wherein her face is lit up with cruel pleasure, and
    she has a beard of sweat
As she has rear-entry intercourse with Vishnu.

The germ of the 580 couplets has passed through a fabulous
    network of tubes.
Strange to think that mind and language can rise from a plate of
    meat!

My tutor lashed it into me with a switch that had my name on it
That every schoolboy is beside himself with envy for his teacher.

But better than "grisly revenge," or any other form of playing to
    the crowd,
Would have been to destroy the boy slowly and privately—by
    means of misapplied pleasure.

Whoever reads more than a dozen ghazals at a time will be over-
    stimulated.
After a certain number of hits, one is simply wasting a precious
    drug.

You should have been a pretty girl, MADRID. The whole world
    might have been spared
All this body-resenting satire in the tone of a parting shot.

I USED TO MANICALLY SLICK MY HAIR BACK

I USED to manically slick my hair back with both hands like a fly.
I used to run my eyebrow antennae through the space between
   my teeth.

I would post myself on a lampshade or on the lip of a lonely girl's
   tub.
I'd sit still, upside down in the curtains, and say in my scheming
   heart:

"Oh, let me just once witness her salty gasp of despair ecstasy!
   Let me
Hear her parched voice CRACK at the first vowel in my secret
   name."

Good times—even if it was the *Jahiliyya*, "the Era of Ignorance."
   Oh, and the
Bedouin poetry I wrote in those days will stand up to a thousand
   readings . . .

But now I know too well that all those sighs and secret names, all
   those
Eye widenings and shudders, they never have anything to do with
   you:—

Say what you like, whatever name she pronounces is His name,
And whatever she pictures in her mind's eye is the IMAGO of the
   Dark God.

TIME WE ROLLED OUT THAT EXQUISITE CARPET

TIME we rolled out that exquisite carpet on which is fiendishly
  worked
The famous interruption of a certain ancient royal wedding
  procession.

The betrothed couple (faces impassive) are both rather past the
  age of thirty.
Yet, boldly naked, with golden bodies, they make for a flashy
  piece of porn.

Her BREASTS are as round and out-thrusting as bells: inflexible
  and superb!
Her bronze nipples are slightly upwards of the out-thrustingmost
  points.

His COCK is curved like a scimitar, and the stylized detailed
  tattoos
Make it look like an arm reaching out from the top of a realistic
  human heart.

Exactly 580 elephants, all of 'em black as umbrella canvas, are
  advancing
In pairs, in full armor, down a thoroughfare cut through the
  jungle.

But obstructing the royal progress is an agèd begging-style poet-
  monk:
Pot-bellied, yogic, eyes crossed, his mind fixed on the JAIN
  religion . . .

And when those regal lovers, sublime as elephants, espied the
  monk,
They alighted from their elephant and said:—

"We must pay our respects to this great soul who is practicing
  harsh austerities!"
And in the only way they knew how, they both tried to *reward* the
  poet-monk . . .

MADRID, this poetry is strange! Who can understand it?
The woman who can understand it has this day herself become a
  bride.

[22 *May* 2004]

LET'S WATCH THIS LIVER-COLORED DEVIL

LET'S watch this liver-colored devil making his way down
    Lovers' Lane.
I want to watch him walk up the wall at the dead end of Lovers'
    Lane.

Let the wicked man and the wicked woman shut their
    complaining mouths.
I shall come round to them presently, shall give them a pond in
    which to mate.

They are dreaming, these uplifters. They look for great things
    from a foolish people.
They are still operating at the level of "the truth shall set you
    free."

Let the poet boy write his own language, and I don't mean his
    mother tongue.
Let him write the language that results from having his precious
    ego SOCKED in the eye.

I used to think I favored the old horsetrader's attitude towards
    beauty:
A squinting, shrewd, and capitalist eye.——*What a lie!*

I came back to NYU and said, "New York: always something to
    look at."
And I meant one enslaving beautygirl after another.

The lewd toddler's a natural thief, and whatever he steals he puts
   in his mouth.
He is perpetually finding pearls to pop into his obscenely white
   oral oyster.

A book is a dead thing. Take it to bed, you're asleep in a minute.
Whereas, if a friend is lying next to you, talking—you stay up all
   the night.

That's the way to write, MADRID! Be like a pillow-talking friend—
A good friend, full of question and answer, head propped up on
   one hand . . .

THEY DO THAT OUT OF ANGER
WHICH WE DO OUT OF LOVE

THEY do that out of anger, which we do out of love. One hates
　　to think of their
Wretched and wretched-making emotions.

I shall denounce them at the top of my voice, though a whisper is
　　sufficient to kill.
I'll right my crooked sword on a fresh anvil and run yelling into
　　their ranks.

I'll say to my modular strophes: Show off the tone in your arms,
　　my girls;
Polish your jewels, use your eyes shooting fire out of cunning and
　　girlish faces.

For my 580 are viral, are contagious, are venereal. Their every
Dimple delivers ordnance; their kissable navels are poisoned.

And today is the last of the month; today I arise and set out for
　　home.
I leave footprints handprints pawprints on the moist sand of the
　　beach.

The sidewinder's pleasant muscle is well fitted to the desert.
Her eggs swivel around inside her like Chinese worry balls.

You say "opposites attract"? Yes, and so does everything else!
You say you hate your own father. Yes, and so does everyone else!

Who taught this young woman to speak? Who taught her this
  English
On which all the secret methods of bragging are perpetually
  brought to bear——?

MADRID, like you, I stand accused of the worst kind of
  recklessness.
I have unleashed upon the world the full force of my infantile
  allure.

I AM YOUR SLAVE NOW DO WHAT I SAY

EASILY impressed is easily fooled, and easily fooled is often. I
  would have my
Coffin carved from a tree in which no songbird ever perched.

What is thy body but a swallowing grave or a chew on a leaf of
  lettuce?
Being a girl has its advantages. I am your slave; now do what I say.

Last day of May but one and it's | the bottom of the ninth. We
Split open the Big Bad Wolf, but the girl inside was very
  strange . . .

The girl who stepped out from that chassis was not | the same as
  the one who went in.
This new one got into Northwestern and majored in International
  Finance.

"The Princess is always in it for the pea"? That's cute, but it's fairly
  misleading.
Verily I say unto you: It's the *pea* that was doing the thinking.

L'objet petit a! L'objet petit a! Uppity little MacGuffin. You
Control the minds of the nation's youth. You lash them ever
  upwards . . .

They all gonna die a thousand years old, rich and covered in sugar.
  But isn't it
Better to eat it like MARLOWE, twenty-nine and a knife in the
  brain——?

Twenty-nine and a knife in the brain before he could lose his lack
of faith.
Oh! if only this same fate could have been visited upon Rochester!

And what is your solution, Shmendrick Numskull?
Sitting there like a mermaid, legs tucked off to the side . . .

You IDENTIFY with Socrates and the Eleatic Stranger—but as for
me,
I'm *through* with these wise men who smile and condescend.

IT IS HALLOWEEN AND MIDNIGHT

I HAVE her love, it's true, but I want her friendship.
What must I do, what spell cast, to have her friendship?

It is Halloween and midnight, and I am surrounded by faulty
    costumes.
Even the couple who came naked were universally faulted.

How tender these young poets are! They can even find a way to
    forgive
Their old high school petting partners who dropped them in
    disgust!

Oh, let my every step be upon a coiled spring. Let me
Leap as high as the PIRATE FLAG of this spiteful young republic.

'Cuz now I've seen everything. Seen the *ringing* TRIUMPH
Of the Self-righteous, Melodramatic, Tasteless and Sophomoric!

And so I took a SLINGSHOT to the alligator in my basement.
I felt safe at the top of the stairs | with my aboriginal weapon.

Braced against my radius, my wrist rocket spoke for me. Ah, that
    eloquent
Schoolboy ricochet, so much better than any boomerang!

How can the mudball, the pea shooter, the flicked thumbtack ever
    compete
With a penny in the crotch of a tense strap of rubber? And how
    can

The King of Pop MICHAEL ROBBINS ever resolve himself into a dew?
Around his head, the nine planets are retrogressing ominously.

And now suddenly there are eight planets. Now seven; now four.
And now once again we must dip | the plastic wand in the soapy
water.

NO MORE EPIGRAMS AGAINST SLUTS

NO more epigrams against sluts. For it galls me to have to hear
These pig men and buccaneers complaining against every little
  unauthorized blowjob.

In my village, hoarding wisdom is forbidden; it's considered
  criminal
To pile up supplies you yourself can never use.

The science of subdivision, of cutting things up smaller and
  smaller,
Tells us there's an almost-eternity between the needleprick and
  the sting.

We put a glue-trapped mouse in a bag, press it still, and give it
  one hammerstroke.
Is no one provoked by the thought we're creating an eternity of
  pain——?

There's another kind of obsessional flirting: got nothing to do
  with sex.
It has to do with trying to toggle the balance of authority.

I have no objection to people's being fascinated by beauty; *I*
  object
To the way people respect it, the way they fall silent in its
  presence.

Men are in all things perverse! They neigh like BUGGERANTHES to
  jam
The three-pronged electrical plug into | the double-dimpled
  outlet.

But where the wire staves of a whisk intersect is filth and
  corrosion's worksite.
Likewise, the shadow one casts on oneself is Wicked Cupid's
  bull's-eye.

HEAVEN HELP THE RIGHT-HANDED MAN
WHO HAS HAD HIS RIGHT HAND CUT OFF

HEAVEN help the right-handed man who has had his right hand
   cut off:
For he must undertake the education of a fool.

A kicking horse made of earth and water can *spill* a man on the
   rocks.
Can pitch him headfirst over the curling spout.

But the sleeper does not die, for sleep is not like death. Or I
   admit
It *is* like death as understood by these cowardly religions.

Little commune child with dirt on your face and dressed in a
   hundred colors!
Come out from that hippy teepee and teach me your household
   rhymes.

For I have ruined my high-stepping new shoes, the wine-colored
   ones, made in Milan.
I used them for tracking back and forth through my portion of
   wedding cake.

And today I see before me, in dazzling motion on their white
   lotus,
Those horrible coupling deities, like a SUNBURST of arms and legs.

And in each of their 580 hands is a different object of religious
    devotion:
A wiggly dagger, a set of heads, a fatty melted pearl . . .

Easy does it, MADRID. Take care whom you denounce. Else
You'll end up in heaven and have to give up this ironizing pose.

I TOO HAVE BEEN TO CANDYLAND

I TOO have been to Candyland, but I found myself missing the
   death cult.
I missed the spectacle of the wounded bones being opened and
   instrumented.

Bill Varner, when he was still just a boy, wrote a stunning line of
   Arabic verse.
He wrote: "The crescent moon is a scimitar; the sun, a severed
   head."

¡Gran cantar! and this, when he still had to keep his books in a
   locker!
And he'd never even held hands with a girl—God! Penn State in
   the 1980s!

In those days, we all sat at the feet of a pig poet, deaf in one ear.
   One of these
Dreadful "white-haired lovers"—oh, but he knew how to touch
   fire to fuse!

That little stick of fire apt to launch a poetic career! But what is it
   now?
Merely a billowing cloud of humidity floating out of a tree.

Every turtle, snake, and bird is "born again"—oh, isn't that so?
   The first time,
Out the fêted cloaca—and the next, through the top of the shell.

The "I" is Greek, the "it" Italian, and Dickinson is our Ghalib. But
   that
Ridiculous piece of dirt you're kissing on can never be anything
   but.

Shut your eyes to what a worm he is, concentrate on his caress—
   but know
Every half-truth is bound to call up its suppressed synoptic
   double.

Close your eyes and moan softly, your head full of packed
   cotton—but know
Every hidden camera's cockpit must one day be delivered of its
   black box.

JAM ME IN HOT HELL

JAM me in hot hell. Make me drive a street-cleaning truck
In the folds of the Devil's anus, but don't make me read all this
  Irish poetry.

I shall drive my flock down to the peat bog, take hold a random
  weed,
Pull it gently until I draw out a whole family of medieval Irish
  criminals.

A black garlic rope hangs from my rafters; it stops just short of
  the floor.
It leads through the ceiling and forms a noose around the ankle of
  a prostitute's bed.

The pulled drawcord on your money pouch is a CHOKE on your
  rival's throat.
So let it be. Let the filthy lucre stew in its own juices.

For if the word *vagina* means sheath, then every baby is a sword.
Preserve us from this line of thinking, O Kūḍalasaṅgamadēva!

O twice-burned lover, risen from the dead with wisdom in your
  mouth,
Today you are looking at a living piece of flesh . . .

I may not seem like much to you now, but you're seeing me after
  the accident.
I know it doesn't matter to yóu, for your love for me is ethereal.

But I am remembering the half hour, the minute, wherein I was
   young and brave and beautiful,
And how all the old guys, no hair and twice my IQ, used to lick
   their lips and stare . . .

Oh, we must go to school to SWIFT, for Swift says there's no
   helping
Hating your neighbor, but you have to be a help to him
   nonetheless.

A MAN AT STOOL IS A LID

A MAN at stool is a lid. Is the top of a canopic jar. Is the
Shabti charged with guarding the sacred pot of royal slops.

Arise, philosopher, and say how it is the box of kitchen matches
Is inscribed with advice so admirably suited to the registered sex
    offender.

The membrane that roots the shell to the turtle is much harder
    than the shell itself.
For the shell is merely stone, but the meat that grips it is rigid
    with FEAR.

Figgy and humid and once widely considered the source of all
    noble enterprise
Is this eyeless bottom-fed river creature that can't bear the least
    little fillip!

If fulfillment lies in harmony, we must harmonize with the
    bouncing ball.
Who makes a mistake will resist in vain the hailshower of broken
    sidewalk.

Shocks my delicacy, these groveling apologies; they chill all social
    intercourse.
They make a good friend of many years' standing as stiff as a
    plastic shoehorn.

But is all this really necessary? Must we open up every egg
And eyeball all that albumen? Are we so wedded to our disgust——?

You can see *my* appetite's whetted for a little sympathetic
 understanding.
You may be sure this poem was not written for the moral know-
 it-alls.

YOU AND I SHOULD HAVE A GREAT RELATIONSHIP

YOU and I should have a great relationship, for you desire to be
  king,
And I, to be the king's indispensable advisor.

Yet, our alliance is not so happy. You object to my hauteur,
And I, to having to listen to your fake poetry.

Every feeble epigram puts my children in hell, makes my
Wedding black, makes my father hate my mother . . .

But when I reveal by my frigid manner any tension or contempt,
You indulge in a monarch's invective against ingratitude.

And so we carry on. But Sa'di says that in debate it is the
Arguments that should stand out, not the veins of the neck.

I with this, and you with me, are burdened until graduation.
'Til that fine day, empty chivalry's bound to lead us a weary
  chase.

Twice my allotment of twice-two years, I've kept company with
  children.
Yóu are cursed with a new set of parents every day . . .

Who? Friend, you. You, whose whole life is a story
Of noble generosity thwarted by insubordination.

MY TUTOR TAUGHT ME ANGRILY

MY tutor taught me angrily, his fists walking about my ears,
That I was to smile with great indulgence on Young Love.

Prepared for me from the Beginning was the poisonously boiling
  water.
Since I see I cannot avoid it, I am working up a thirst.

My mother's skin and my father's beard are a comfort to me in
  dreams.
I spend all my waking life trying to improve on those pleasures.

Immaturity's not knowing your motives? No, it's something
  rather worse.
Immaturity is not knowing that your motives are transparent.

A glass ball is a good stop to the mouth of a glass bottle. I can't
  stop
Lightly drumming my nails on the floor of this paper cup.

A beautiful girl—*beautiful!*—despite her buck teeth. She says,
With her eyes on fire, that she's never felt this way before;—

She's never felt this way before, but she's only nineteen.
Get *over* yourself, MADRID. She's never felt any way before.

WHOEVER WORRIES TOO MUCH
ABOUT BEING BELIEVED

SHALL I write the little platitude poem that will save somebody's
   life?
I can no more write that poem than I can think rice into my bowl.

If GLAMOR's the soul of poetry, then I say: *Poetry, do your job.* We
   must
Liberate the human love of licking boots . . .

Whoever worries too much about being believed will only end up
   lying.
In trying to persuade our parents, we forget everything we know.

That suasion and credit are only the millionth part of the poet's
   task.
That poets lay their goldenmost eggs on stacks of rotting bricks.

The worst of them is in my house, corrupting my servants.
At night, I hear her in the stairwell, hear her groaning with rude
   pleasure.

Oh, she's a big hit with the ladies, this modern Artful Dodger!
   With her
Newsboy cap and her gallantry and her long-sleeve war-eagle
   tattoos!

But the bruise on a fruit marks the spot where the biting teeth
   will turn back.
Yet, it's not the teeth, it's the MIND that relies on "voluptuous
   resistance."

In better days, I called all infants "the crying people." I called
Christ "that Bedouin philosopher"; I shook my fist at the
   oncoming traffic . . .

But now, the piston action in the cylinders is suffering a loss of
   pressure.
I can just barely open up my unoiled mechanical wings . . .

Oh, look! the monster is *crying!* Come, we must dry his tears.
Let me go. I wanna wipe his tears with my BOOT SOLE.

IT IS A PERFECT DAY AND I MUST WASTE IT

IT is a perfect day and I must waste it. I have to sit in a vault
Beneath the palace, counting other people's money.

My JOB is teaching virgins apostrophe and comma.
But, for this all-consuming work, I'm paid in poetry.

I trust the poetry of the naked people, river culture art. I like the
Shamanistic animal poetry of the uninhibited hunter-gatherer.

But when I see cameras going up at every crossroads, I foresee
The approach of universal colonoscopy.

Universal colonoscopy!—the very word is like a knell: It means the
End of all pleasure that doesn't know how to defend itself in
    court.

And so it'll be in my apartment that I write my dissertation.
I hold my pen up to the light and squint into its fuselage . . .

Strange! that you can see people so much better through
    binoculars
Than by sitting directly across from them on the train;—

That's because people behave naturally when they don't know
    they're being watched.
It turns out the same is true for material objects.

Nay, speak not lightly of my association with that famous jewel-
   like beauty.
For it is on her behalf I have learned to speak in verse.

I have the two-thousand-year-old classics, the old books; I have
   the
Three-thousand-year-old classics for companions;—

But never have I known any satisfaction better than this.
The memory of a star-crossed Platonic friendship.

THE HAVING A RICH STOCK OF WINE

MY judges have bruised their gavels, and now my punishment is
  fast upon me.
I have to play fosterparent to a superabsorbent baby born out of
  wedlock.

O Lilac! you loveable roll of toddling paper towels! Come and let
  me teach you
The art of poetry: the radix and the omega thereof.

For I am eager to pleasure babies; I am eager because I trust
Their approbation is a litmus for human goodness . . .

The ghost delusion is founded on a five-year-old's self-
  centeredness.
With regard to the works of the FATHER, we are most of us five
  years old.

We imagine malice flowing through objects, vengeance in the
  speed of light; we think
The color wheel is against us, and the list of simple machines.
  And indeed

The human spine is a priming rod, but the brain is not the bullet.
Lunatic, can't you see you've holstered your six-guns upside
  down?

We are all of us walking in blood. You want to know just how much,
Stand on your head, you'll feel the HEAT of it as it gushes into your face.

Who trains herself to bottle her passions will one day have quite the wine cellar.
And, in truth, the having a rich stock of wine is itself a heady drug.

At the end of the *Iliad*, Hektor, Breaker of Horses, loses his nerve.
And at the end of the *Ramayana*, King Rama doubts his Sita . . .

—Conclusions evilly disappointing! But this is exactly why
Homer and Valmiki are considered artists of the first rank.

THE ALL-CRUSHING OR RATHER
ALL-TO-NOTHING-CRUSHING KANT

OH der alleszermalmende Kant! The all-crushing
Or rather all-to-nothing-crushing KANT.

I don't want that guy to be right, 'cuz if he's right, I'm a *fool*.
A fool—and a bad role model for my students.

I took a bottle, mashed its bottom into a thick coat of paint.
Then I STAMPED a ring of kisses into the palm of my hand.

I did wrong to try to understand these sensualist children.
In them the light is neither wave nor particle.

Ninety percent of these living angels'll never hold a job.
They're all gonna have to *walk* from Chicago to Los Angeles.

Tarantula has to shed its skin. Dude, I seen 'em do it!
The upshot's like a new paintjob on a Formula One racecar.

But the replacement parts are twice the cost of the original
   equipment.
The disambiguation doesn't even begin to disambiguate.

So I started looking at my own legs as if they were a girl's.
Gotta say: *I like what I see.*

DELINQUENCY gets an uptick every time I buy a book. Every
   Time I grind a coffee bean, I release an African leprechaun . . .

But I am too milde. Reach me my scourge againe. I have to
Skilsaw a ghazal out of this sheet of galvanized steel.

GIRLS WHO ARE UNFAITHFUL AND
AT THE SAME TIME RELENTLESSLY HONEST

GIRLS who are unfaithful and at the same time relentlessly
  honest
Are not operating in accord with the Darker-Than-Any-Mystery.

Only she who is relentlessly faithful and meanwhile full of lies
Can be said to be in accord with the Darker-Than-Any-Mystery.

The MADNESS OF LOVE takes many forms. In me, it's the illusion
I am Abul-Majd Majdud ibn Adam Sanai Ghaznavi.

Hé wanted the whole universe to be an unconjugated verb.
I won't say which, I'll let you guess. *Ha!*—right on the first try.

Yet, to me, "love" is not even a noun; it's merely a case inflection.
Any name in the D-L triple-X can be inflected for *Ishq-e-Majazi*.

So, don't say "God is great." Say "God is glamour"—it's what you
  mean.
The Almighty *bottoms* the bhakti. GOD is the ultimate TOP. And
  that's why

The Tibetan Fuckmaster King says if a halt were put to all
  coupling,
The human race would end, not after a generation, but that very
  instant.

And if I am impenetrable in this and my other verses,
It is only because you can't penetrate | a wall that is not there.

I am the poet MARDUD; I had no childhood. Whoever wants
To get at my meaning will have to turn her back on her childhood.

I LIKE THE IDEA OF THE KICKBACK

I LIKE the idea of the kickback, the reward of devilish loyalty.
I hope to receive my own manly comeuppance, lying flat on my
front.

Fussy girl! you say you must see a boy's face if you're to
pronounce on his beauty?
The INITIATE can judge a beauty just from a glance at the back of
the neck!

The left hand wants to get into the act? wants to rival the right in
cunning?
No, it just wants to be able to undo the hooks that meet at a
woman's spine.

To disarticulate thóse hooks is a task that asks some skill. For the
interlocking
Fangs of the snake are settled like a screw rusted into its nut.

Sublime are these vibrating metallic wasps—sisters to spark and
to dragonfly.
But who can compete with the stings released from every cut into
Cousin Onion?

In the case of trancey poetry, there's a great difference between
eye and ear.
Pioneer, they are both of them corrupt, but I say the latter is the
less so.

MADRID is assembling a ladder. He means to ascend and make a
  speech.
He will make a fine valedictorian at the gallows' summit . . .

BECAUSE IT LOOKED LIKE A CASTLE IN SPAIN

BECAUSE it looked like a castle in Spain, I had to book "31" for
  extraction.
Melissa had to stand behind me and brace my head in the crook of
  her arm:—

She had to rock my jaw back and forth, like drawing a nail out a
  floorboard.
A big nail! but, oddly, I was as comfortable as a kitten being
  petted.

There it is, you either relate with the cat or you relate with the
  petting hand:
Oh! the hand suddenly deprived of the pleasure of *giving* pleasure!

I won't praise rationality, that bootlicker to the passions.
Better praise the passions directly—and in a language they can
  understand.

In the volcanic heart of a wood louse is a snowflake-shaped
  candelabrum:
An ever-diminishing crystal of original sin!

And now we are on an open raft on the surface of Jupiter.
We are riding on a twelve-hundred-mile-deep ocean of liquid
  hydrogen.

We are directly under the canopy of the GREAT RED SPOT. It's like
  being
Under a turning parasol that takes up half the sky.

A slowly turning parasol made of water-damaged silk with rolling Octagons of light opening and closing along the edge.

I SHALL MAKE ME A BOOK

WHAT a pleasure, to explore by myself these virgin haunts of the
  Muses!
What a joy to kneel and drink deep at these completely
  un-fucked-with fountains!

I shall make me a book that can only be read by natural light. A
  book wherein
The Devil will have his due, and the Angel his comeuppance.

O tiny rhombus of glitter stuck to the cheek of my belovèd!
You were born in a good hour to come to such an auspicious end!

I am like a girl in love, a girl from India or ancient Greece.
  Indeed,
I am physically shriveling like the sexy witch in the *Pharmaceutria*.

Sa'di, that saintly sheik, says if a woman speaks good things,
You are not to think homely or not homely, but marry her.

My dragon-bearded tetrameters! how dare you speak of marriage?
What need have you or I for a polluted exchange of covenants?

Am I supernaturally eloquent? Yes, if you'll give me a minute. I
  have to
Confer with my favorite author: John of Patmos.

MADRID is just now examining Scripture with certain of the Lord's
  children.
Pull up a chair—

For, if hearing a single verse of the Diamond Sutra was enough to
  enlighten Hui Neng,
Imagine what listening to the whole thing'll do for a bright guy
  like you.

WHEN CLOUD-COLORED LIGHT PLAYS
ON THE BODY'S NAKED SURFACE

WHEN cloud-colored light plays on the body's naked surface,
The definition, the shadows ravish the eye.

Perhaps that's why Vātsyāyana, immortal author of the *Kama
Useless*,
Recommends not poetry but *neumond* starlight to the man-about-
town.

Very few women have seen my body—and, in a sense, not even
they.
For I am recently translated into | an hitherto-unthinkable beauty.

The ELEVEN DIRECTIONS are mine: north and south and the other
two, and
The ones between, and up and down, and even the broken axle is
mine.

But, rather than see my fractious name carved on the front of
Butler Library,
I would gladly hear it hissed in uttermost scorn by the girl from
Rose Apple Tree Island.

NADYA! you know those paintings with railroad tracks and
vanishing points?
You shoot off a gun in one of those paintings, the bullet goes to
the vanishing point.

ALL MY LIFE I'VE BEEN TOLD YOU MUST
TAKE THE BABY FROM THE CROCODILE

ALL my life I've been told you must take the baby from the
crocodile and give it back to its mother.
You must never take it away from its mother and give it back to
the crocodile!!

I walk into the library. I see a hole in the line of books. I fit my
book into the hole
And slam it into place.

Every star on the US flag is a piece of Japanese cabinetry. Is a white
lacquer box
Openable on every side but one.

Who's locked out at this wedding? Only the bride and the groom.
And who was that child sent sprawling rather than let him catch
the bouquet?

I admire the duck. He sits up straight. He zooms on top of the
water.
And he has a rubber effigy beloved of children . . .

Pygmalion had the right idea. He deserved his reward. For he had
a statue but he wanted a girl;
Most guys have a girl but they want a statue.

MADRID, who you trying to fool with all this talk of animals and
statues?
You are yourself a box out of which a pair of newlyweds are locked.

I AM NO LONGER CUT TO THE HEART

I AM no longer cut to the heart to watch her laughing with my
    rival.
Any man who gives her pleasure I consider my emissary.

She said to me proudly, "I mean to ruin you for other women."
    She was what
These moral morons call "a consummate technician."

Here's that boy with demon sideburns and slicked-back black hair
And a shirt like from the bodyshop, complete with cotton
    racing-stripe namepatch.

I say to him: "Approach me, my child, and thou shalt be my
    chosen delegate,
For thou art seventeen feet tall and tricked out with a half mile of
    tattoos.

Go to the girl with the gemmy blue eyes and glossy asymmetrical
    hair.
Speak gorgeous English into her glasses, give her something to
    scheme on . . . "

9-28-05, and it's raining in Ukrainian Village. The ambulance
    parked
Outside this joint has a crest of waterferns exploding out the top.

Load me into that ambulance, my friends. And if you bump my
    dreaming head,
Tell the driver not to worry, for I have no physical sensations . . .

Oh, GOD! the pleasure's too much, MADRID! I'm dying, *dying!* But
   if I have to
Die of unwanted pleasure, all I ask is that I not die alone.

THAT STARLIGHT-EMBROIDERED SASH

OH, it was a medical FACT that he was gorgeous.
Skin, hair, teeth—all precious metals.

And who could resist his flamenco-inflected English? Gay or
straight,
No man could withstand the headlong strength of the MANGET.

Ah, those ancient magic horseshoes! They knew how to get things
done.
As you pressed the extremities together, came a point where one
would violently flip.

So, let's up on our stiletti, gentlemen! Let us not for a moment
forget
How *winning* it is when a sexy young thing is clumsy on her heels.

Let's hear it for all licking and biting. Let's hear it for *Bend Over,
Boyfriend*.
Let's hear it for those black plastic belts with rows of silver
pyramids!

I say we will have no more marriages! I want to teach and be
taught.
I want to be kitted out for every possible erotic contingency.

I want to say: "Today she is Queen of Beauty, with a tiara to rival
the sun,—
A long green gown and a bathing suit with the #4 tag still on!

She has defeated the Vietnamese sexpot and the seven-foot blonde
  in slacks:
They have to stand back and watch the bouquet bounce into her
  happy hands!

That bundled and crackling rosebush! That starlight-embroidered
  sash!
And that final walk down the runway, punctuáted with camera
  flash!

Stand aside, you lesser beauties, for MADRID is coming through!
Miss Teen Queen Photogenic, soon to be seen on pay-per-view!"

WHAT WITH THIS NEW BODY

I AM impatient, I am irreverent, I am addicted to giving pleasure.
You could say I haven't the scholar's cast of mind.

I wouldn't even let 'em put a cast on my broken arm! I said:
  Better my bones
Divert their course around the stones in the river of life.

It is not for me to subtract from their stock of therapeutic
  laughter.
Only, release me from the obligation to egg them on.

People like poets to be good-looking? I do my best not to
  disappoint.
And what with this new body, I am become a blip on the gaydar.

Let's flip through *The Devil's Dictionary*, see if we can find a nudist.
  Ah, here he is:
"A forty-year-old guy, quite naked, except for his horn-rimmed
  glasses."

Conspiratorial Rat says, "I am a schemer, through and through."
He says with a wink: "Whoever spares my life is complicit with
  the bubonic plague."

HINDUISM! that fractal religion with gods sticking out of the gods!
Every time you open the faucet, you get a sink full of gods.

MADRID, do you not see your poetry gives comfort to the wicked? It does give comfort to the wicked—but it also makes wiser the wise.

HELLO YOU LOVELY LITTLE ROSE

HELLO, you lovely little rose, unmeaning, useless to me. And
   luck
To the beard of the beautyboy who's waiting for you in the street!

Luck to his beard, for he has dipped his cup in a tank full of
   sounding whales.
He loves that plangent and echoing music that can be stored in a
   glass of water.

The dropped opera house chandelier has the look of a sunken
   Navy destroyer.
The ones still floating on their chains are more like dew-shot
   caterpillar tents.

A pleasant-conceited boy with a dog and a flashlight will soon
   discover
He can tease the dog by making a hand of GOD drop from the
   ceiling.

Though the poet's medium's mere shadow, he still likes to make
   the dog duck.
Then he'll make the duck into a naked woman, and himself into a
   beautiful girl;—

"You see I have a curly elaboration of hair: beautiful, and
   beautifully bobbed.
You see I keep it all wild above and straight-edged along the
   bottom.

And now I work my fingers, curved and raking, in. And I
Ruffle the whole mass, after which it collapses into a new shape."

The two halves of a halved grape are the RUNE for the Ass of the
   Future.
Whatever woman wants to press wine from thát grape | will have
   need of her high-heeled shoes.

THESE WERE NOT BORN TO BE LOVERS

THESE were not born to be lovers, for they are very unlike the
 Great,
Who take off their clothes with every confidence that their bodies
 will "fill the eye."

We have no word for the provocative dimples at a young woman's
 lower back.
And we have no *adequate* word for the curves into which | her
 turquoise pendant hangs.

But if evocative words could be coined, perhaps a spell could be
 cast
By whose agency we might part the seam in our masculine
 cocoon.

O traveler, is that smoke on the wall there, or only the smoke's
 shadow?
The trick answer is you can have it either way—but it'll cost you
 a little savvy.

Tell you something about beauty. You get for free what others
 must pay for.
That's why it's an INSULT when somebody sticks their finger in your
 face and says to you: *You're gonna pay*.

But in the Christian high school where I work, I am exempt from
 every stricture.
I am free to play Lady Godiva riding a vibrator down the hall.

Oh, violet thong underwear, exquisite and exquisitely visible!
Oh, shiny black leather riding crop and delectable jut of the hip!

It's about time MADRID turned a few heads. Just look at him:
  you could read
The small print on your marriage contract by the light coming off
  his face.

TO NADYA

TO the girl with too many beautiful penguins, good morning.
Good morning, you supreme essence of female beauty, if not of
  vitality.

Girl from all ghazal poetry. Beautiful Nadya, virtuous Nadya.
Little Nadya Pencilthwapper, our sometime sister, now our
  queen.

This morning I kiss your apple cheeks. Your strawberry nose,
  your purple eyelids.
We have a busy day ahead of us. We have to teach Machiavelli for
  good.

Nadya, why does not everyone desire you? Why are you not
  swarmed with love?
Your virtue is a five-mile-high geyser of liquid nitrogen.

Nadya, I have my eye on you. And even when you were a child,
I commissioned that little boy with his paper valentine . . .

But last night I looked through a second-floor window, saw a rack
  of hanging copper pans.
The window panel was divvied up into neat black rectangles . . .

So, Nadya Mgongo, let's go out there again tonight.
The firelit copper pans will give you joy.

I'M MY OWN GAL I ANSWER TO NOBODY

I'M my own gal—I answer to nobody.
Let those beautyboys, gloomy as eagles, do their worst.

People are not lovable? Well, that's why I don't love.
And if I'm still "vulnerable to circumstance," it's no matter.

The terrible cataloguer of lusts, who holds up every lurid detail
At the end of a pair of tweezers, may proceed in peace:—

Let him write his dirty *Book of Boys and Girls*—I'll not complain.
And if I crave an untroubled repose, I'll confer with my pillow.

And if somebody asks my secret, I'll say: "Friends, it's just
    nothing.
I have neither beauty nor courage nor wisdom; all that I have

Is a firm devotion to kindness, to the bankrupting of all revenge,
To the point where I never say to anybody, *Just get over it.*

And as for love and the act of love, let me (like Lolita) be true to
    my Dick.
Let me bring comfort to my Nadya in her unhappy time . . . "

And now MADRID's ascending into heaven! Here's our chance to
    look up his dress!
Oh, but God! the thing I see there—! It's like a shark shaking the
    life out of the back wheel of a tractor!

ROUTE 50 DAMEN TO 35TH/ARCHER ORANGE LINE

ROUTE 50: Damen: to 35th/Archer Orange Line. October 12th, 2007. And coming into the home stretch.

This. Is Insanity. Doors open on the left | at Insanity. They have put a padlock on Hell, and I—am trying out combinations.

Here come Hippy Santa Claus with his overalls and plastic flute. Warm as a bruise, I eye the entrance to Armadillo and Napkin.

This day let armored insect advance its bebarbative suit. It tears nor the case, nor the bagged and beautiful muscle . . .

Beautiful Lady, show me your muscle. (Show me your muscle, Beautiful Lady, and show me your holster, guy with a gun!)

Officer Hunkasaurus is stripped to the duty belt. And now they're painting him with wrestling oil to make him even sexier—!

His task is to shimmy up to the top of that flagpole. God! it's like a heat wave in Syria. Just look at these suffering birds:—

Common-as-popcorn hopping sparrows with their mouths all hanging open. It lets the overeager heat out like the screaming end of a teapot.

Poor little perching birds, boiling like the blob of water that precedes the flame up the cubical kitchen matchstick!

Going to Ife, we face Ife; coming back, we still face the same way. The skull is too small for the brain. The tines on this fork are all splayed out.

MADRID, whose magic song made a mountain fold its tiny arms, must now fold in *his* arms the black fluffpuff | that floats at the top of the mountain.

THE MILK ONE

HE has no gift for friendship, for he is void of all curiosity. Or
rather,
He's only interested in matters touching the Lord Hamlet himself.

He was born in a lab whose walls were lined with giant, steamy
jars
Of the milk of the various mammals, from the milk of camels to
the milk of men.

Pig milk, monkey milk, rat milk. Dog and cat milk, and the milk
of whales.
The milk of the duck-billed platypus and that | of the
platitudinous buck.

The thick red milk of the vampire bat. And the black milk of the
black bear.
—A backlit wall of bottles, ranged from commonplace to rare!—

There was stallion milk and rooster, anaconda milk and shark;
There was tarantula milk, Venus flytrap, and that | of the barking
aardvark lark.

And he would have been perfectly normal, would have grown up
socially adroit,
But he stripped the sheet off a drinking straw, took a blade, and
shaped a point;—

And he syringed into his body a few drops from every jar,
Fell in the floor and spoke languages he had never heard before.

He spoke Titmouse. He spoke Miaow. He spoke Moo and Gnu
 and Ha.
He spoke three kinds of Chickenhawk and the thirty dialects of
 Baa.

And from that day to this, MARDUD's been lost in the zoo:
A cautionary tale for whoever knows how to read the clues.

IT IS NOT FOR DOGS TO TELL
THEIR MASTERS WHAT TO DO

IT is not for dogs to tell their masters what to do. It is not for me
To wipe my arse—it is for my manservants to perform this act.

The CATARACT cannot be negotiated. Our little white paper boat
Will ship water, will be upended at the first cleft in the rocks.

And I, too, have been capsized, wrecked | by a single chisel-
    edged eyebrow. It's how
Many a middle-aged woman retains | the charm of her Scottish
    girlhood.

And the heavenly sage CHRIS CRAWFORD, who is now a snake
    and now a bird—
And now something neither snake nor bird, for which the
    language has no expression—

Has entered upon a LUSCIOUS THEME dear to all degenerates.
He says it's easy to summon courage—harder to say why.

He does not believe in the Precepts! His inner Chamber of Deputies
Is full of wild fox spirits and iconoclast bodhisattvas!

But I'll not go to Jeta Forest—or, going, I shall not stay. I would
Sooner alter the personal name of a TALISMANIC OBJECT.

This sword has a *personal name*. This chariot, this wine goblet.
This GLOCK 9 and this shining pair | of hemostatic forceps.

But the PRECEPTS are coming to getcha. They are mocking when
  they say:
Cock and cunt will come together, check them how you may.

"Cock and cunt will come together"? *Cock a fucking ear!*
Whoever *has* an ear, let him hear what the Spirit saith unto the
  churches.

RHYMES

THE door is rusted; the wall is clean. Red, yellow, orange, green.
Many a maiden has come between | a gentleman and his luck.

Red, yellow, orange, red. Never you mind what the minister said.
You live, you die, and then you're dead—so go ahead and be evil.

The smallest cage in the human zoo. Red, yellow, orange, blue.
Ready or not, it's time we do | away with all this uplift.

So, purple-orange, black and white. Oh say can you see by the
traffic light?
Your kid can try with all his might, he'll never do long division.

The 400 Blows was about a kid. Red, yellow, orange, red.
It could have been me and yet instead | they set the controls for
tragic.

Oh orange, orange, yellow, black. A passionate fuck to patch the
crack.
A narrative designed to attract | children and other retards.

Regarding yours of March 18: yellow, yellow, orange, green.
Most of these citizens aren't really mean, just reckless with
people's feelings.

Oh green, green, *que te quiere* green. God got giddy on Halloween.
Jebus, the Jolly Ghost, and He | put a razor blade in the apple.
Now,

You're on your own and off your meds. Greens and yellows, blues and reds.

It's only with certain groups of friends | you dare undermine the uplift.

So, purple-orange, yellow-blue. Polly, gimme your answer true.

I order demand and require that you | tear it, little parrot.

So, let's hear it all for the CASH MACHINE. Purple-orange, yellow, green.

Dirty Bomb and Laser Beam | are here to collect the rent.

HONEYMOON

I WAS Mike and she was Jenn—just like everybody else. The boy
   is sick
And the girl wants to make love? Good story of first love.

We pay nine bucks to sit in a theater, yet it goes on all around us
   for free.
O sand flea with barbed-wire eyebrows! stay away from my
   waning honeymoon!

The shutter closes, but the film won't advance (hey ho, the
   shudder!).
I suppose if we'd never had sex before, tonight would be the very
   first time.

Of the many things in this world that are not love at first sight,
   one is playing chess
With a hostile alcoholic Math PhD who happens to be the father
   of the bride.

Oh, this crowded bed by the exit, and the door left carelessly
   unlocked.
And the whole place lit by that faraway moon, with its submarines
   under the ice;—

EUROPA! with its robot submarines looking for life under miles of
   ice. But even if they
Find some little piece of life, it's just gonna be a bunch of
   amoebas.

And as for erotic agonies? Well, for every good one, there are a
million bad.
It's raining outside, and it's sad in here. Hey kid, don't take it so
hard.

Hey kid, I'll give you a bottle of beer if you'll go play with that
someplace else.
Or you want money? Go over to the dresser and reach me my
wallet out of my clothes.

But the girl by the pool will have gone home by now. The surfers
have all come ashore.
That "virgin isle of healing mud" turned out to be industrial waste.

The girl by the pool? Gone home. The surfers? Missing or
drowned.
The alarm clock's hammer is poised on its bell. Young Love has
had its say.

¡Qué bárbara! eh? How these child actors have to sacrifice their
youth. And for what?
Just one more summer comedy | where the cunning little jerk
gets the hot girl with the million IQ.

NOW THAT I KNOW I AM TO BE DESTROYED BY A SEVENTEEN-YEAR-OLD GIRL

NOW that I know I am to be destroyed by a seventeen-year-old
  girl,
Doesn't matter what I do. I can drink poison if I want. Can run a
  nail into my neck.

Nothing gonna happen to me. For I am fated to be destroyed
By a CHILD, an illiterate girl with cartoon characters on her panties.

I have absolutely nothing to worry about! I can lean out the door
  of the helicopter.
I'm as invulnerable as Rāvaṇa. Only a GIRL can cut off my head.

I need no weapons, no suit of armor | to fight a soot-spitting
  dragon.
A dragon the size of a Gothic cathedral, whose slobber *smokes* with
  bacteria.

I can fight GOJIRA bare-handed—or only armed with a roll of
  toilet paper.
Doesn't matter; I cannot be injured. My NEMESIS is only a girl.

No "trifling in a double sense" here; I am to be killed by a high
  school senior.
A girl whose hair bounces as she jumps up and down, or runs up
  the stairs of the post office . . .

There's an Arabic letter, same thing as our "r"—in calligraphic
  script,
It is a flipped or rotated CIPHER for my ruiner's right eyebrow.

So, she's easy to spot, easy to evade. And I know just what not to
  do.
At ease in my mind, I set out from Corinth; they are waiting for
  me in Thebes . . .

I am an INDESTRUCTIBLE EAGLE. I am the *invincible* poet MARDUD.
I lay me down, I fall asleep as soon | as my head hits the pillow.

THE 1897 EDITION OF
THE SEARS ROEBUCK CATALOGUE

HEART full of desire? Heart too soft.
Eyeball always thirsty? So water the little mint plant.

Are not all women beautiful? Babies seem to think so.
But I'm not *like* the other boys—I don't go by looks.

I've *read* my country's Lucretius—a 700-page facsimile
Of the 1897 edition of the Sears Roebuck catalogue.

But, having searched that cornucopia, that surgical tray of tools,
Having surveyed the 10,000 objects, I closed the beautiful book.

In your culture, do you have a word for people who don't learn
    from experience?
SRIKANTH REDDY's written a treatise on it. Sonneteer, read it and
    weep.

Yo los bautizo a ustedes con agua; él, con el Espíritu Santo.
And if even thát's not enough for you, you ought to listen to the
    poet HAFEZ.

He says you should be like an oyster. "If they cut your head, give
    them a pearl."
I approve the poet Hafez for he speaks with loving, perverted
    sweetness . . .

And VIRTUE is not what we thought it was. It has nothing whatever
    to do
With the pursuit of Athletic Athena or Jackrabbit Aphrodite.

So, twinkle, twinkle, little planet. Don't pretend to understand it.
It's just a streak of gold or silver through a panel of unreflecting
    black.

A streak of gold or silver through a FIELD of ribonucleic black!
    Don't let it
Make what was only a lack of light into an annihilating void.

IF I AM A TOTAL WASHOUT AS A LOVER (AND I AM)

IF I am a total washout as a lover (and I am),
I want to know: Where was my teacher?

If I have no skills, no sense of adventure, if I'm hemmed in by
   mere convention,
I want to know: *Where was my teacher?*

Where was my teacher when, as a boy, I tried to flirt with those
   Mormon girls?
Where was he when one of those girls had white legs and boots
   black as India ink——?

My teacher, where was he? where? when I stayed up late with that
   Jehovah's Witness!
She said, "I'm so óver Jehovah," but you could tell that she wasn't
   really.

And what about that Jewish Orthodox? And her dress with the
   tiny white dots?
That girl had phone sex with God! She was friends-with-privileges
   with GOD!

Teacher, you were neglectful. You didn't guide my faltering steps.
   You thought
"The girl thing" would take care of itself. You left me to my own
   devices . . .

And so I wound up married at twenty-two—to none other than
    Lopez the Cobra!
That Catholic icon with her gold *crucifijo* and her Paolo Friere
    politics!

Why is the world so sexy? Where do religious babies come from?
Teacher, if ever I got any answers, I had to grow 'em all by
    myself.

And now I have a homeschool PhD in Scheming and Self-
    Restraint.
Yesterday, I unrolled my prayer rug, and listened for a voice from
    the Unseen. It said:——

Be not ashamed of the male gaze, MARDUD. *Defend it from these saintly
    persons*
Who believe that no one should ever be allowed to look at anyone else.

MARDUD, *your mouth is wont to gush lies; be not dismayed that no one
    believes you.*
Yet, tell out all the truths it took you thirty years to learn.

*And if you would speak the Ultimate Truth, I will tell it you, once and
    for all.*
*It's that the trick is not so much to get rid of your vices, but to turn them
    to good account.*

THE MEDICAL EXPERT HELD THE FLOOR

DISCUSSION is their wont. Discussion have I none. I was
Silent in assembly at the crucial moment.

The MEDICAL EXPERT held the floor. He was holding forth on
   Woman.
Every syllable out of his mouth hurt my ears.

Every *word* made my sweet little sleeping kitty get worms. Made
   WORMS
Play pinochle on-a my snout.

So, let my bulubwalata be blunt, that my protection magic be
   keen.
May I be vouchsafed the privilege of CATALYTIC STASIS.

'Cuz castling's a good move—protects your King—but comes a
   point
When you must learn to use the King as an attack piece.

The KING has bad weather today; he has to pay his taxes.
And yóu have to pay the tax on being good-looking . . .

In this generation, the RIVAL is always a Katie or a Caitlin,
Always a hundred-pound gamine with a lot of eye makeup . . .

But cunning and eloquence in children speak the company of
   slaves.
A CHILD should be as plain and to the purpose as a soldier.

MADRID is smiling in his sleep; we mustn't interrupt him.
He is dreaming he is bargaining for souls.

AT NIGHT THERE ARE MILLIONS OF SUNS

AT night, there are millions of suns; in the daytime, only one.
Like with so many things, we adore the light that happens to be
  nearest.

Dust, which takes root on vacancy, is the unacknowledged
  substrate
Of all the monosyllabic things in human nature.

They cannot deny you water, but they can deny you every
  kindness.
And this is why I prefer—and more than prefer—to live in a state
  of thirst.

To teach is to go back in time; to learn is to visit the future. But to
Stand there like a mule, not a thought in your head—that's "living
  in the moment."

I was wrong to ask your opinion when all I wanted was praise.
You were wrong to take a tone of patient instruction.

We have a tradition in our poetry that babies give off light.
Actually, the naked human body gives off darkness.

The poem says Adam went to sleep and his Father played doctor.
  True enough,—
But at that point, the chronology goes astray.

The correct sequence should be sleep, strange dream and woman-
out-of-nowhere,—
And only *then* does the ungainly rib find its way out of Adam's
side.

Indeed, the magic wand thing is always on backwards. You touch
a thing
With the wand, yes—but it's *you* who are magically changed.

Oh, when I die, cut a hole in my foot and let all the water run out
of me.
Then at my funeral you can take me out and STRIKE me on the side
of the box.

THE MASCULINE GOD OF PASSIVE LONGING
IS RIDING THE HEAD OF A FLOWER

THE masculine god of passive longing is riding the head of a
flower. He fits
An arrow into the corner of his bow and draws back his right fist
to his ear.

27 August 2009, last days of forty. With the *Fifth Decad* of THE
CANTOS about to begin,
I must find a way to trick my grief.

I must find a way to trick my grief, to outstrip it—or dodge it as
one dodges a cop.
For is this done by wreathing myself seven times round with
elegant quickness.

The WHITE ELEPHANT is my witness. I have set up a table out front
Of the INFORMATION KIOSK that can be found at the top of his spine.

Spieglein, Spieglein an der Wand, wer ist die schönste im ganzen Land?
I'll run
An extension cord up to the sun. Robe and tassel, cap and gun.

Not saying I'm a good person. I deserve what punishments I get.
And yet
When it comes to men and women I have my head screwed on
straight.

I know how to draw a BEADED CORD through a justbarelybig-
  enough aperture
And then make the sound of thát into | a new kind of prosody.

Where the Monongahela River meets the mighty Allegheny
Is a jewelrybox metropolis that dare not speak its name.

And it's obvious the Founding Fathers found | the very thing they
  were looking for.
The busywork and distraction that come from living in a hostile
  environment.

And the NOSTRIL is a great conduit for the Temporality-Boggling
  Dharma.
But, Bhagavan, I am *quits* with the Temporality-Boggling Dharma.

Halloween last, I got trashed, wound up at the wrong party,
  fingerfucked a Sleestak.
Captain Lou Albano shook his finger in my face, but I flicked my
  skirt and ran around and jammed a fork in an avocado.

Well, cock-a-doodle-doo, Sacagawea! Fuss factor fifty, and you
  coulda got us all killed.
You know many and many an astonishing thing. But now the
  CHILD wants to lecture *you* for a while.

SEND ME UP THE WRONG SIDE OF
MOTH'S-EYEBROW MOUNTAIN

HEY, high-ranking god unjustly demoted at the recentmost
  change of cards. You
Who beat STARS from Arabic jacket-iron, take command of my
  battering radius.

For these unmanned flights to Mars will never turn up the least
  dot of water.
For how can anyone turn up the water without first laying hands
  on the spigot?

The bigotry of these ineducable children is like the magnetosphere
  of the sun.
GASEOUS GIANTS patrol the darkness under sway of that mysterious
  force.

The PRIME NUMBERS, too, are subject to gravity; they, too, have a
  galactic center. That
Pulsing zero, indivisible—with nullity and emptiness for all!

The DOLL I had as a child was nothing if not anatomically correct.
  When I looked in its
Pants, the feeling I had was indescribable revulsion.

Barbie, don't trust that Ken. He may be good with shapes and
  colors,
But insofar as you let him drive the car—that's how far you drive
  up the tree.

In due time we shall see for ourselves who is prophet and who is
fool.
We'll see who has to COOK THE BOOKS to show a return on owner's
equity.

So, send me up the wrong side of Moth's-Eyebrow Mountain; set
me down in a sinking place
Where I'll need all this equipment I don't even know how to use
to make it up the first ice wall!

And now MADRID is wearing a spacesuit. He forged it in this
poem's first couplet. And now
He is splashing around in shattered glass with a family of sexy
robots.

WE HAVE LEFT THE WORLD TO BE SAVED
BY PERSONS UNFIT TO LIVE IN IT

MY brothers, we have left the world to be saved by persons unfit
    to live in it.
The depressed will never save the world, for they | unconsciously
    long to be rid of it.

The CONSTITUTIONALLY DEPRESSED are in the grip of an ax-grinding
    saturnine arrogance.
They can only detect intelligence in that which | conduces to the
    zero sum.

No wonder they love their SUNZI, that much-translated Daoist war
    manual.
The world's only instruction book | on how to be passive
    aggressive.

O ye of little tact. How you long to hear confessions. You want to
    go on national
Television and dish out the advice . . .

My brothers, we are different. We respect our materials. When
    issuing
A travelers' advisory the *last* thing we want to see is tears.

We must wrest the world from the depressed, from those who
    put stock in repentance.
For they cannot see how repentance is merely a piece of sacred
    theater.

Trembling, pedantic, they step up to the plate and solemnly take
a vow.
They think, *Dreamland starts now. For I have a piece of paper.*

Mama didn't love me don't matter no more—for I have a piece of paper.
And hand in hand, out of Eden they take | their slow and solitary
way . . .

Wake up, Homer. C'mon, Homer: rise and shine. For the HUMAN
BOTCH
Cannot grow a new head, nor should this be asked of him.

The cracked ego cannot be patched. It is too late for the
individual.
In China we say, "Three Buddhas and two sticks of incense." It
means none for you.

FUCK BUDDHA I'M BUDDHA NOBODY'S BUDDHA QUIT TALKING ABOUT BUDDHA

FUCK Buddha, I'm Buddha, nobody's Buddha, quit talking about
  Buddha.
You can't intimidate *me* with your Thangka-toy halo.

You can't intimidate me with your kneeling animals, your
  "journey," your treasure words.
For I am just returned from beyond the endurable limits of human
  wisdom.

I walked on the bottom of a swimming pool. Saw giraffe-skin
  patterns of light.
Saw for myself what the light spelled out, and here is what I now
  know:

That gravity is not love. No; nor explosiveness, strife. Let me not
To the marriage of true minds admit Empedocles.

That mirrors are for seeing 'round corners. They are not for
  looking straight on.
That's why whoever looks into a mirror sees something other than
  a face.

And that you are all *sanpaku*—for you buy into all that sex talk.
  Body parts
Hunting body parts—and then you're shocked it's not enough.

You should walk a poolbottom. David Hockney has painted this. You'll
Shuck all that Buddha talk. You'll send up little bubbles . . .

And perhaps you'll shed a tear for your babbling younger self.
Don't be afraid to cry. For crying replenishes the pool. And
   indeed

The Maitreya Buddha MARDUD has no quarrel with sentimental
   tears.
He says the harm only comes in when we try to defend them.

THE SUMMER OF 1976

AH, these Hellenic honeycomb clusters of different-colored sea-
 facing cubes!
Since this one was built on a ROCK WALL, no two houses are on the
 same street.

There áre no streets: only terracotta stairs whose gracefully
 wrought swash railings
Hold BANKS of potted succulents in place at the edge of every step.

To gét anywhere you have to be prepared to go through each
 other's houses. The only
Person allowed any privacy is whoever lives at the very top.

And would you play upon me? Would you seem to know my
 stops? There is
Much music in this little organ—yet cannot you make it speak.

I shall post a Greek in the boat. A freethinking philosophical
 Greek.
For, unique among pre-Socratics, this one RESPECTED the Barbarian
 mind.

He *refused* to think rings around people. He said intelligence is
 almost all myth. He likened
The shape and color of lightning to a track of thought through the
 human brain.

He disdained all keys and locks. He RELEGATED all such
To the involutions of the labyrinth containing the Minotaur's
    mighty opposite.

You know about that embarrassing opposite. Head of a man, body
    of a bull.
There's one on the cover of this new translation of *Also sprach
    Zarathustra*.

But we must go back in time even further: to the summer of 1976,
When Dixie and Nestor had just put in | the pool in the back
    yard.

And now I see EMERGING from the much-agitated water
A dripping troop of children tanned the color of leather belts!

It is my TRIBE climbing out from a smoking hole on the side of
    Parnassus.
And there among them is the greatest living space poet, Ted
    Greenwald!

Ted Greenwald, Ted Greenwald! I send you this hymenopterous
    poem
From my apartment on the kangaroo side of a golden Australian
    penny.

WHAT IS THAT FIERY BALL IN THE SKY

WHAT is that fiery ball in the sky? And how is it we can feel it?
How can we stand on the front lawn and endure | the heat of a
    nuclear explosion?

What is this thing called light? And how can it be kindled?
How can these meaningless insects casually traffic in cold fusion?

The illusion of understanding these things prevents our
    transportation.
And, too, we are distracted by | the shadow of the money
    tweezers.

See the MONEY TWEEZERS threateningly perched on that nearby
    ranch-style fence!
Thieving money tweezers! Always on the lookout for nesting
    materials!

That's just part óf it, Valerius. Life in the tall grass.
The redwing blackbird trills in vain for the Pharmaceuticals
    major.

What's pleasure? I mean what is it besides the gratification of the
    senses?
Why should it be such a satisfaction to travel incognito? And
    indeed,

The SCANNING ELECTRON MICROPHONE cannot detect my movements.
For my mission is to alter the course | of human personality.

Babe, don't touch the curls. And, oh, for Godzilla's sake,
Do not be disposed to criticize | where you do not understand.

Come, fiery ball in the sky. Come, firefly and redwing blackbird.
And even you, Pharmacy major, come and join me in this
   spaceship.

For when the sun goes SUPERGIANT, the going gets good on TITAN:
The only nearby atmosphere | like that of the primordial earth.

AFTER SI NISI NUM AND NE EVERY ALI- GOES AWAY

AFTER *si*, *nisi*, *num*, and *ne*, every *ali-* goes away. But after
Seeing Nadya in her shirt, my every nerve was on alert.

GUSTAVE FLAUBERT lay in a revery. Wrote a snarky book for every
Dixie, Daisy, Ray, and Sue. *Le Dictionnaire des idées reçues.*

The MOVIES, boy, they'll ruin you. Best cool your jets. But there's
   no
Point in taking a Sex Ed. course, 'cuz they don't teach you *jack*.

"Didn't shut Milton down, won't shut me."—Such is my new
   motto.
And why *not* play the lotto? Only costs me a mouthful of air.

My rare little Russian camera | padding across the floor!
In her panties and ephemera, she could spark a Trojan War.

Who spoke to ya, Monkey? I know your estrogen and tricks. What
   the
Rumpus Schmitty McSchmittfuck is your problem?

And here's little Mr Ticklebug with his idiotic sidekick. Watch 'em
Run up a hill and swat a gong in *hommage* to the three little
   witches!

How is it these privileged mean girls always have such expressive
   faces?
Mr Ticklebug!! Look out for that upright | fox with his tail shot
   off!

Gustave Flaubert leapt out his chair, rewrote the whole enchilada.
Bury the Muse. After all, this is | the Century of Overreaction.

BURY THE MUSE; she is dead. Her braids have come undone. You
  don't
Wanna be that girl. Believe me, you don't . . .

No motion has she now, no force. She neither sees nor hears.
Rolled 'round in Earth's diurnal course—with rocks and stones
  and bears.

BALLAD

I SPUR my horse to the river. To the river I spur my horse.
Because my horse is invisible, I see beneath me a curious thing.

Because my horse is invisible, and because I am totally naked,
I see beneath me a mighty afflatus | and hoofprints mashed in the
grass.

I spur my horse to the river. To the river I spur my horse.
We FORD the river as best we can, horseshoulder-deep in the
drink.

Because my horse is invisible, I see beneath me a horse-shaped
hollow:
I have never once seen my horse and now here | is its
photographic negative.

A moving void in the river. And the motes in the muddy green
Rushing against its thoracic hollowplace are deflected in all
directions.

Because I am totally naked, I have stolen an invisible horse.
I spur my horse to the river. I am in flight from the authorities.

"Counsel uses a term with which | the Bench is unfamiliar."
I spur my horse to the river. The boy in the bright blue jeans.

Because I am totally naked, Counsel uses a term.
We ford the river, the muddy green. I'm all eyeball.

And high up on the embankment: a formidable radio tower.
An erector set tower, stuck all over | with shamanistic drums.

I spur my horse to the river. To the river I spur my horse.
Let me remember the things I love. The mourners all are
   singing . . .

Counsel uses a term. I am looking through a shower door. I am
Horseshoulder-deep in a river churning, churning with invisible
   horses.

I'm a KNIGHT'S MOVE away from my target. My target, the radio
   drums.
Shoefly, dragonfly. Churning with invisible horses.

An invisible horse will leap. Will strike and then depart. But his
Favorite trick is spring out of the way: spring and reveal a ROOK.

I'm all eyeball. And you have maintained your composure, so
   long as
Nobody saw your naked fangs, nor caught a stripe off your
   horsewhip . . .

You've maintained your composure. But EQUIPOISE is better:
You get to keep your sense of humor. I spur my horse to the
   river.

O YOU BEAUTIFUL YOUNG READERS OF POETRY

O YOU beautiful young readers of poetry, and especially you
   beautiful young men—
Have pity on my dried-up talent. Forgive my reveling here in this
   light.

I have lived one hundred ninety-five years, each one boring-er
   than the last. Yóu
Have all the satisfactions of anonymity before you.

Love for that luminescent beauty has made me quite transparent.
   When her
Rays pass through me, I have to take care not to focus them on a
   FUSE.

What *is* Christianity, anyway? Is it a theological tractate? Or
   merely
Whatever answers the needs of people standing at gravesites—?

Every grave has a silver lining. That boy for whom I pined
Was nothing more than a clump of earth from the lip of such a
   grave.

I am guilty; I am cause of guilt; but I am also guilt's cure:
For whoever takes one look at me immediately feels a
   comparative saint.

The taint of the PSEUDO-MARTYR is upon me; I won't deny it. My
   injured mouth
Is bleeding away like a gaudy Mexican crucifix;—

MADRID, you effervescing piece of fuckass magma! anyone can
  see
How much better this poetry would be if it were written by a
  twenty-five-year-old punk.

APOCALYPSE

HAVING read their terrible poems, having hated, I rose terribly
  upwards.
My flesh—out of blind hatred—exploded off my bones like bats.

Like bats in a panic, my crawling fat PRECIPITATED off my skeleton.
My suddenly naked scaffolding RESONATED with rage.

And I saw below me the earth was opening; the oceans were
  unraveling.
And I saw rushing into the reactor core were freight trains and
  ships.

And I saw the consonantal sprocket come loose from the vowel
  chain.
And I saw anastomosing galaxies collapse.

And I heard the language God uses to scold the incorrigible
  angels:
A set of rhythmic humming pulses, half meter, half dementia.

And the smoke enveloping my understanding all blew away;—
And I stared into the face of the static GODHEAD;—

And I and you and he/she/it—all at once, we closed our books.
And peace reasserted its rights then. Peace and clouds and
  dreamless sleep.

INDEX OF FIRST LINES

JAM me in hot hell. Make me drive a street-cleaning truck   38

LET'S watch this liver-colored devil making his way down Lovers' Lane.   24

MOST living creatures leave no ghost, and even if they do it's totally useless.   8
MY brothers, we have left the world to be saved by persons unfit to live in it.   98
MY judges have bruised their gavels, and now my punishment is fast upon me.   48
MY tutor taught me angrily, his fists walking about my ears,   43

NO more epigrams against sluts. For it galls me to have to hear   32
NOW that I know I am to be destroyed by a seventeen-year-old girl,   84

O YOU beautiful young readers of poetry, and especially you beautiful young men—   110
OF the many hymns to the goddess Kali, only one is worthy a poet's respect.   20
OH der alleszermalmende Kant! The all-crushing   50
OH, it was a medical FACT that he was gorgeous.   64

ROUTE 50: Damen: to 35th/Archer Orange Line.   74

SHALL I write the little platitude poem that will save somebody's life?   44
SHE wants to know what I'm looking at, so I tell her I'm looking at her body.   16

THE door is rusted; the wall is clean. Red, yellow, orange, green.   80
THE masculine god of passive longing is riding the head of a flower. He fits   94
THE unit of wine is the cup. Of LOVE, the unit is the kiss. *That's here*.   9
THEIR fulminations are mere theater, and their offended morals, smoke.   12
THESE were not born to be lovers, for they are very unlike the Great,   70
THEY do that out of anger, which we do out of love. One hates to think of their   26
THEY have built a public fountain with the stones they threw at my father.   5
TIME we rolled out that exquisite carpet on which is fiendishly worked   22
TO the girl with too many beautiful penguins, good morning.   72

WAR-weary general, manfully squinting into the sunlight,   14
WHAT a pleasure, to explore by myself these virgin haunts of the Muses!   58
WHAT is that fiery ball in the sky? And how is it we can feel it?   104
WHEN cloud-colored light plays on the body's naked surface,   60

YOU and I should have a great relationship, for you desire to be king,   42

ACKNOWLEDGMENTS

Grateful acknowledgment is made to the editors of the following journals in which some of these poems first appeared: *AGNI Online*, *Another Chicago Magazine*, *Antennae*, *Blackbox Manifold* (UK), *Boston Review*, *Cincinnati Review*, *The Claudius App*, *Copper Nickel*, *Fence*, *FlashPoint*, *Folio*, *Forklift, Ohio*, *Gulf Coast*, *The Hat*, *HTMLGIANT*, *iO*, *Iowa Review*, *Juked*, *LIT*, *MAKE*, *Milk*, *1913: A Journal of Forms*, *Orbis* (UK), *PANK*, *Pif*, *Poetry*, *Shampoo*, *6X6*, *Typo*, *WEB CONJUNCTIONS*, *Word For/Word*, and *Zoland Poetry*.

Many thanks also to the editors of Cosa Nostra Editions, who published some of these poems in a chapbook, *The 580 Strophes*.

Anthony Madrid was born in 1968, raised in Maryland. He lives in Chicago with Nadya Pittendrigh.